THE YOUNG PIANIST'S LIBRARY

No. 1A

MW01098513

FROM BACH TO BARTOK

ORIGINAL PIANO PIECES BY THE MASTERS

VOLUME A

Selected and Edited by

DENES AGAY

DANCE SONG

From Johann Sebastian Bach's
"Notebook for Anna Magdalena"

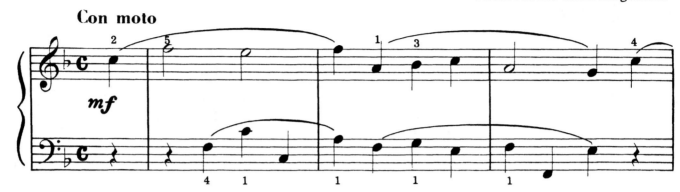

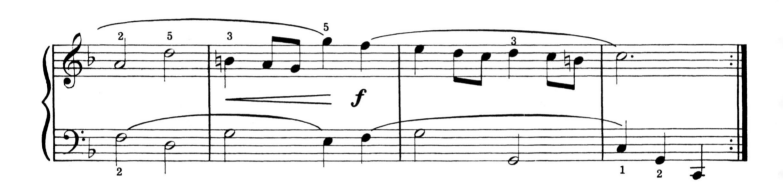

CHORALE

From Johann Sebastian Bach's
"Notebook for Anna Magdalena"

TM 21674-23

MINUET

From Johann Sebastian Bach's
"Notebook for Anna Magdalena"

Moderato

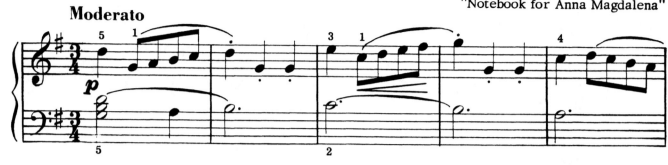

PASSEPIED

GEORGE FREDERICK HANDEL

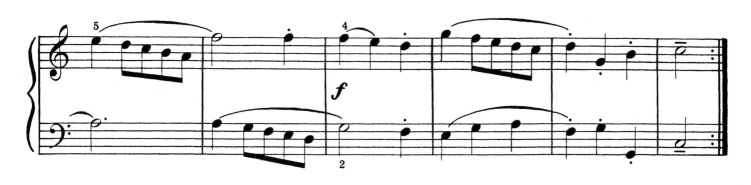

TM 21674-23

RONDINO

JEAN PHILIPPE RAMEAU

RUSTIC DANCE
(Schwaebisch)

Animato; ben ritmo

JOHANN CHRISTOPH FRIEDRICH BACH

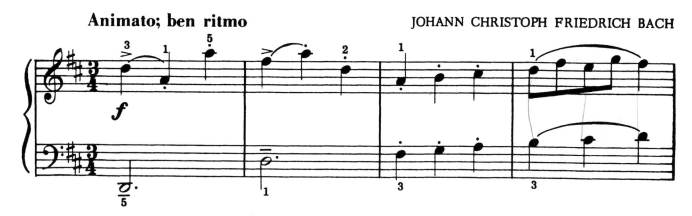

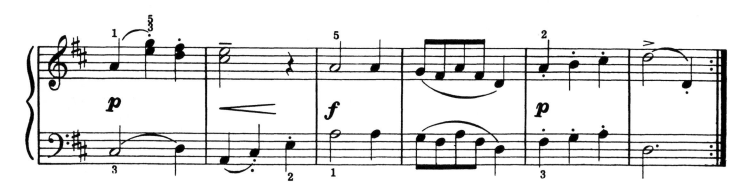

NANNERL'S MINUET

From Leopold Mozart's
"Notebook for Nannerl"

Andantino

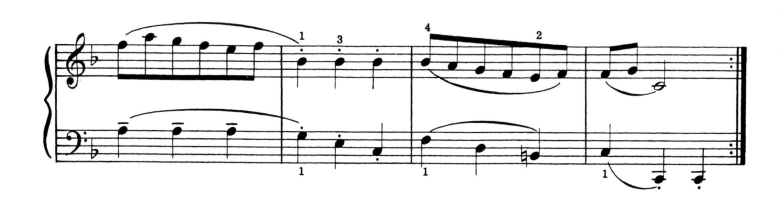

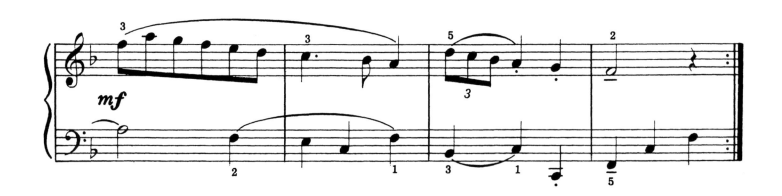

BOURRÉE

From Leopold Mozart's "Notebook for Wolfgang"

Vivace

AIR

JOSEPH HAYDN

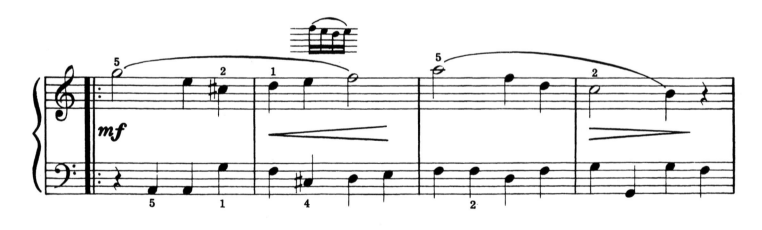

COUNTRY DANCE

Allegretto

JOSEPH HAYDN

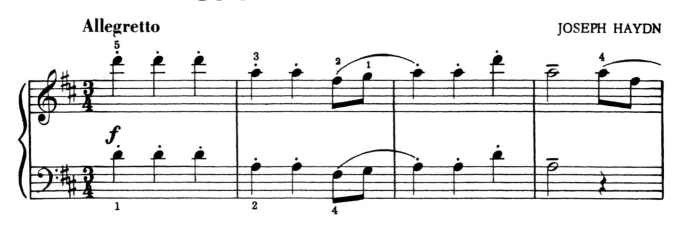

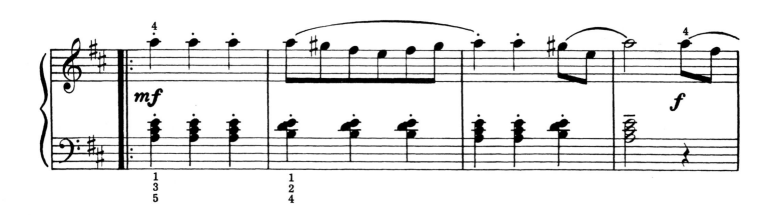

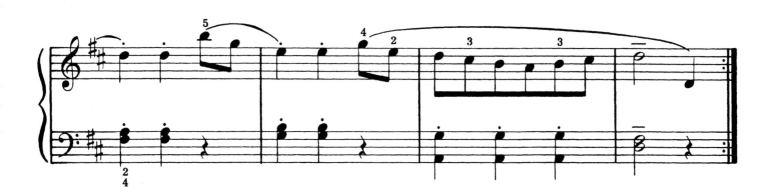

TM 21674-23

BAGATELLE

ANTONIO DIABELLI

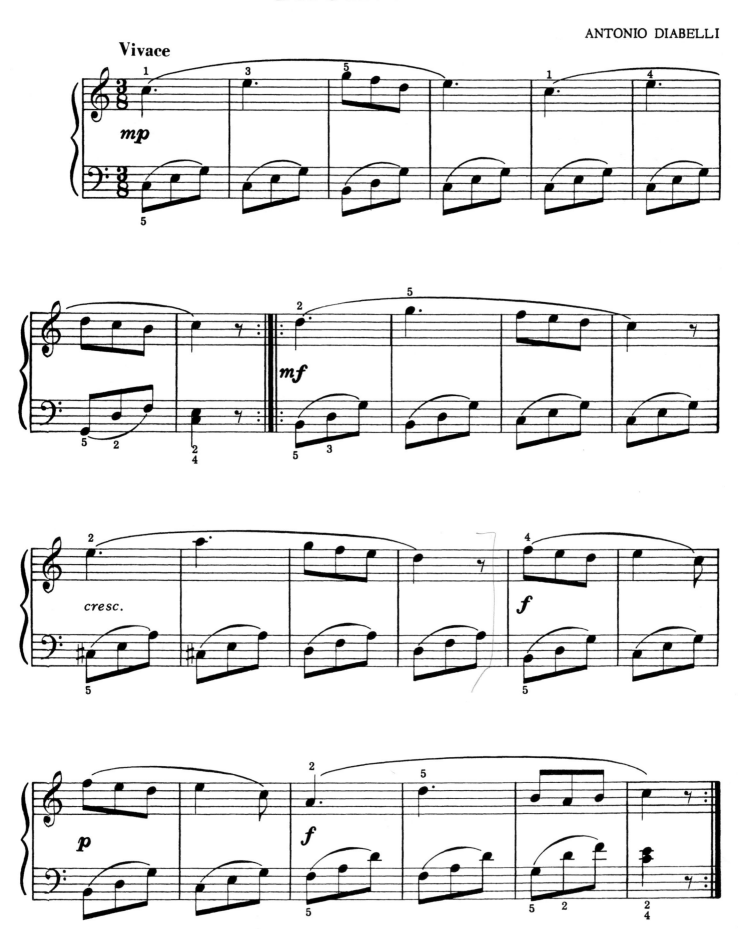

ARIETTA

WOLFGANG AMADEUS MOZART

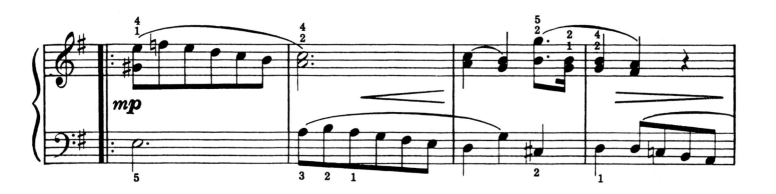

* Original in A♭

TM 21674-23

ALLEGRO

WOLFGANG AMADEUS MOZART

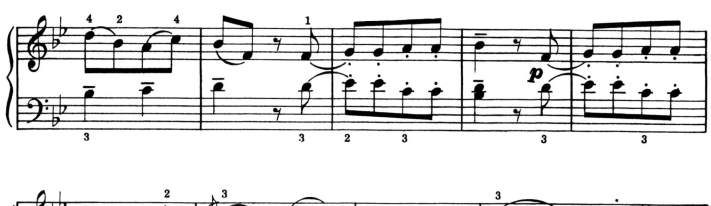

RUSSIAN FOLK TUNE

Allegretto

LUDWIG VAN BEETHOVEN

HAPPY MOMENTS

DANIEL GOTTLOB TÜRK

A BIT OF SADNESS

DANIEL GOTTLOB TÜRK

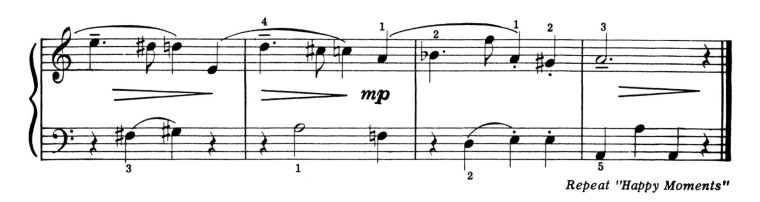

Repeat "Happy Moments"

ÉCOSSAISE

JOHANN NEPOMUK HUMMEL

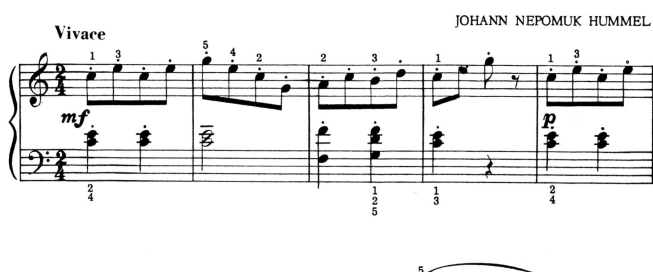

TM 21674-23

GERMAN DANCE

LUDWIG VAN BEETHOVEN

Moderato

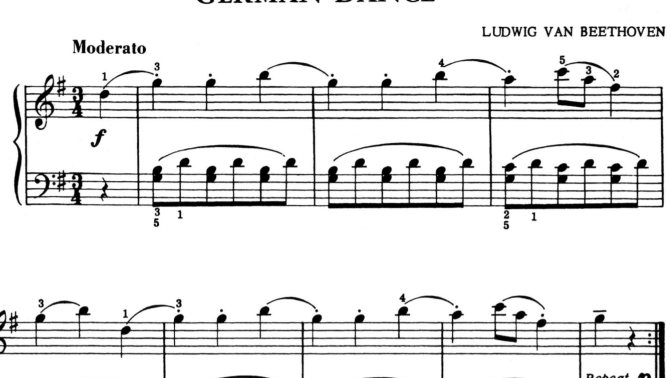

SOLDIERS' MARCH

ROBERT SCHUMANN

TM 21674-23

WALKING PIECE

IGOR STRAVINSKY

Andantino

POLKA

DMITRI KABALEVSKY

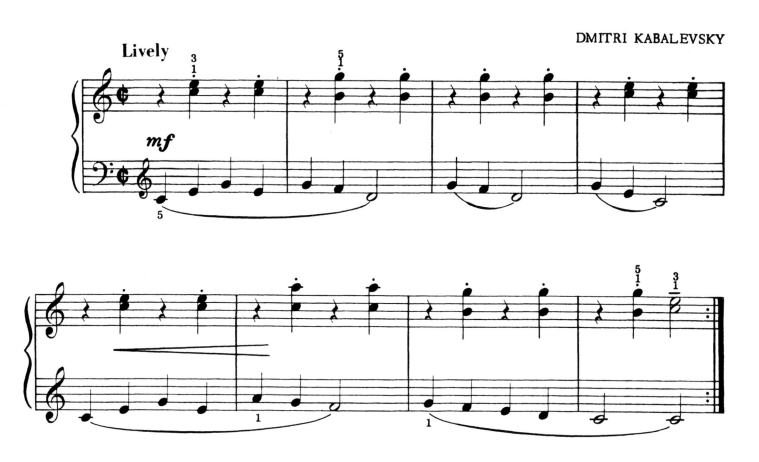

LULLABY

DMITRI KABALEVSKY

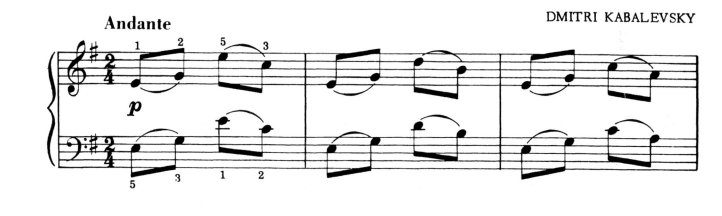

TM 21674-23

FUNNY DIALOGUE

DMITRI KABALEVSKY

VILLAGE DANCE

BÉLA BARTÓK

MORNING SONG

BÉLA BARTÓK

Moderato

THE SHEPHERD'S TUNE

BÉLA BARTOK

Andantino